The Frui Diet Cookbook

Learn How to Adopt a Fruit Based Eating Lifestyle with Nutritious Recipes

Emily Smith

A GUIDE TO EATING FRUITS FOR TOTAL WELL-BEING

"Every step towards a healthier life is a pledge to nurture your body, mind, and spirit for lasting well-being."

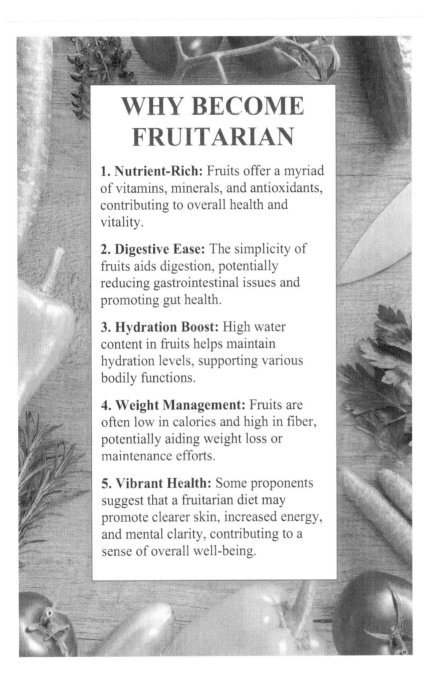

WHY BECOME FRUITARIAN

1. Nutrient-Rich: Fruits offer a myriad of vitamins, minerals, and antioxidants, contributing to overall health and vitality.

2. Digestive Ease: The simplicity of fruits aids digestion, potentially reducing gastrointestinal issues and promoting gut health.

3. Hydration Boost: High water content in fruits helps maintain hydration levels, supporting various bodily functions.

4. Weight Management: Fruits are often low in calories and high in fiber, potentially aiding weight loss or maintenance efforts.

5. Vibrant Health: Some proponents suggest that a fruitarian diet may promote clearer skin, increased energy, and mental clarity, contributing to a sense of overall well-being.

Table of contents

6

INTRODUCTION TO FRUITARIANISM

Fruitarianism represents a dietary lifestyle centered around the consumption of predominantly fruits, alongside select plant-based foods like nuts, seeds, and certain vegetables.

Rooted in the principle of consuming foods without causing harm to plants, it embodies a philosophy that extends beyond mere sustenance, aiming to harmonize with nature, promote health, and reduce environmental impact.

At its core, the concept of fruitarianism emphasizes consuming fruits that can be harvested without causing harm to the plant itself. This means opting for fruits that naturally fall from trees or bushes, such as apples, oranges, berries, and avocados, and excluding foods like vegetables that require uprooting or harming the plant.

Some practitioners also consume nuts, seeds, and certain non-sweet fruits like tomatoes, cucumbers, and bell peppers, provided they align with the principle of minimal harm to the plant.

Advocates of the fruitarian diet often cite its alignment with natural living and sustainability as driving factors. By adhering to a diet that primarily involves the consumption of fruits, proponents aim to minimize their ecological footprint, believing that such a diet is more in harmony with the environment and the natural order of life.

Fruitarianism is not just about food; it's a lifestyle choice that extends to ethical and environmental considerations. Followers of this diet often adopt a mindful approach to living, seeking to create minimal impact on the planet and practicing principles of eco-consciousness in various aspects of their lives.

One of the core beliefs among fruitarians is that a diet primarily composed of fruits can contribute to overall health and well-being.

They highlight the nutritional benefits of fruits, which are rich in vitamins, minerals, antioxidants, and fiber. Proponents of this lifestyle claim that consuming a variety of fruits provides the body with essential nutrients and supports optimal health, promoting benefits such as increased energy, improved digestion, and better skin health.

However, it's important to acknowledge the potential challenges and considerations associated with adopting a fruitarian diet. Critics of this lifestyle often point out the risk of nutritional deficiencies, particularly in protein, calcium, iron, vitamin B12, and omega-3 fatty acids, which are crucial for overall health. This diet can be restrictive and may require careful planning to ensure adequate nutrient intake.

Transitioning to a fruitarian diet requires thoughtful consideration and may involve a gradual adjustment period. It's advisable for individuals considering this lifestyle to consult with a healthcare professional or a registered dietitian to ensure they meet their nutritional needs and mitigate potential health risks.

In essence, fruitarianism represents more than just a dietary choice; it's a lifestyle guided by principles of harmony with nature, sustainability, and ethical considerations.

While proponents advocate for its potential health benefits and alignment with environmental consciousness, individuals must approach this lifestyle change mindfully, understanding its limitations, potential challenges, and the necessity for careful nutritional planning.

Adopting the Fruitarian Diet can be a life changing decision against diseases

CHAPTER ONE

Understanding the Fruitarian Diet

The Fruitarian Diet stands as a distinctive dietary lifestyle centered on the consumption of predominantly raw fruits, supplemented by nuts, seeds, and select vegetables. Rooted in principles of natural living and ethical eating, this dietary choice embodies a philosophy that extends beyond mere sustenance, aiming to align with nature while promoting health and well-being.

Principles of Fruitarianism

At its core, the Fruitarian Diet advocates consuming fruits that can be harvested without causing harm to the plant itself. This includes fruits that naturally fall from trees or bushes, emphasizing a diet that minimizes harm to plants and aligns with the principles of eco-consciousness.

Proponents avoid foods that involve uprooting or harming the plant, excluding vegetables, grains, legumes, and animal products.

Benefits of Fruitarianism

Proponents of the Fruitarian Diet emphasize its alignment with natural living and sustainability. By focusing on fruits that can be obtained without harming plants, adherents believe they are reducing their ecological footprint and contributing to environmental conservation.

Furthermore, fruits are rich in essential nutrients, vitamins, minerals, antioxidants, and fiber, which supporters claim provide numerous health benefits. These include increased energy levels, improved digestion, better skin health, and overall well-being.

Potential Challenges of the Fruitarian Diet

While the Fruitarian Diet boasts potential health benefits and an eco-friendly ethos, it also poses several challenges. Critics highlight concerns about potential nutritional deficiencies, particularly in protein, calcium, iron, vitamin B12, and omega-3 fatty acids, which are essential for optimal health. The restrictive nature of the diet and the potential difficulty in meeting daily nutritional requirements present significant challenges.

Furthermore, transitioning to and maintaining a fruitarian lifestyle may require careful planning and diligent sourcing of high-quality, ripe fruits.

Considerations for Adopting a Fruitarian Diet

Transitioning to a fruitarian lifestyle necessitates thoughtful consideration and mindful planning. It's advisable for individuals contemplating this diet to consult with a healthcare professional or a registered dietitian to ensure they meet their nutritional needs and mitigate potential health risks. Careful meal planning and supplementation might be necessary to address possible nutrient deficiencies.

In essence, the Fruitarian Diet represents a unique dietary choice that integrates ethical considerations, sustainability, and natural living principles.

While proponents highlight its potential health benefits and alignment with eco-consciousness, individuals should approach this dietary lifestyle change with caution, understanding its limitations, potential challenges, and the importance of adequate nutritional planning to support overall health and well-being.

Transitioning to a Fruitarian Lifestyle

Transitioning to a fruitarian lifestyle is a significant dietary shift that requires careful consideration and a gradual adjustment process.

Here are some tips for individuals looking to gradually adopt and adjust to the fruitarian diet:

1. Educate Yourself

Start by thoroughly understanding the principles and guidelines of the fruitarian diet. Learn about the types of fruits allowed, the philosophy behind the diet, and the potential benefits and challenges associated with this lifestyle.

2. Gradual Transition

Consider a gradual transition rather than an abrupt dietary shift. Start by incorporating more fruits into your daily meals while gradually reducing the consumption of non-fruity foods. Gradually phasing out foods that don't align with the fruitarian principles can help your body adapt.

3. Diversify Your Fruits

Explore a wide variety of fruits to ensure a diverse nutrient intake. Experiment with different types of sweet fruits like apples, bananas, mangoes, and berries, as well as non-sweet fruits like tomatoes, avocados, cucumbers, and bell peppers.

4. Balanced Nutrition

While fruits offer numerous nutrients, it's essential to ensure a balanced intake. Pay attention to incorporating a variety of fruits to cover essential nutrients like vitamins, minerals, antioxidants, and fiber.

Consider consulting a healthcare professional or a registered dietitian to develop a meal plan that meets your nutritional needs.

5. Hydration and Water-Rich Fruits

Ensure adequate hydration by consuming water-rich fruits. Fruits like watermelon, oranges, and grapes can contribute to your daily water intake, supporting overall hydration levels.

6. Mindful Eating

Practice mindful eating by paying attention to hunger cues and the body's response to different fruits. Listen to your body and its reactions as you introduce new fruits, noting any sensitivities or digestive changes.

7. Support and Community

Connect with others who follow or are transitioning to a fruitarian lifestyle. Seek support from online communities, forums, or local groups where you can share experiences, tips, and recipes with like-minded individuals.

8. Patience and Adaptation

Be patient with your body's adjustment process. Adaptation to a new dietary lifestyle takes time, and your body may require an adjustment period. Be observant of any changes in energy levels, digestion, or overall well-being and make necessary adjustments accordingly.

9. Sustainability and Sourcing

Opt for locally sourced, organic, and seasonal fruits whenever possible. Supporting sustainable agriculture practices aligns with the ethos of the fruitarian lifestyle and ensures high-quality produce.

Transitioning to a fruitarian lifestyle is a personal journey that requires mindfulness, patience, and a balanced approach to ensure adequate nutrition and well-being.

Gradual changes and a focus on a diverse array of fruits can help ease the transition while supporting your body's adjustment to this dietary approach.

Health Considerations

Exploring the health considerations of a fruitarian diet involves understanding both the potential nutritional benefits and risks associated with this dietary approach.

Potential Nutritional Benefits:

1. Nutrient-Dense Diet: Fruits are packed with essential nutrients like vitamins (such as vitamin C, vitamin A, and various B vitamins), minerals (including potassium, magnesium, and folate), antioxidants, and fiber, contributing to overall health and well-being.

2. Hydration and Water Content: Many fruits have high water content, aiding in hydration and supporting bodily functions. Water-rich fruits like watermelon and oranges contribute to daily water intake.

3. Antioxidant Power: Fruits are rich in antioxidants, which help combat oxidative stress, reduce inflammation, and support the body's defense against chronic diseases.

4. Digestive Health: The fiber content in fruits can promote digestive health by aiding in regular bowel movements and maintaining gut health.

Potential Risks and Nutritional Concerns:

1. Nutritional Deficiencies: A fruitarian diet may lack certain essential nutrients, including protein, calcium, iron, vitamin B12, and omega-3 fatty acids. Inadequate intake of these nutrients can lead to deficiencies and health complications.

2. Protein Intake: Fruits generally have low protein content, and relying solely on fruits may make it challenging to meet daily protein needs, potentially leading to muscle loss and weakness.

3. Iron and Calcium Absorption: Some fruits contain compounds that can hinder the absorption of iron and calcium. This could contribute to deficiencies in these minerals, affecting bone health and overall energy levels.

4. Vitamin B12 Deficiency: Vitamin B12 is primarily found in animal products, and its absence in a fruitarian diet can lead to deficiencies, potentially causing neurological and hematological issues.

5. Omega-3 Fatty Acids: Fruits lack omega-3 fatty acids, essential for brain health and reducing inflammation. The absence of these fats might pose risks for cardiovascular health and cognitive function.

Balancing a Fruitarian Diet:

To mitigate potential risks associated with a fruitarian diet, individuals should consider:

- **Supplementation:** Consulting a healthcare professional or dietitian for appropriate supplementation of essential nutrients lacking in the diet.

- **Diverse Fruit Intake:** Ensuring a wide variety of fruits to cover a spectrum of nutrients.

- **Monitoring Health:** Regular health check-ups to monitor nutrient levels and overall health.

- **Balanced Approach:** Combining a fruitarian diet with select nutrient-dense foods to address potential deficiencies.

Understanding both the benefits and potential risks of a fruitarian diet is essential for individuals considering this lifestyle. Careful planning, supplementation when necessary, and monitoring health can help maintain a balanced approach to ensure nutritional adequacy while following a fruit-based dietary pattern.

EATING FRUITS EVERYDAY WILL KEEP THE DOCTOR AWAY.

THEY ARE NUTRIENT RICH AND EASY TO SOURCE

CHAPTER 2

Getting Started with Fruitarian Eating

 Embarking on a fruitarian eating journey involves a thoughtful approach to incorporate and adapt to a diet primarily centered around fruits while minimizing harm to plants.

Here's a guide on getting started with fruitarian eating:

Transitioning to a fruitarian lifestyle begins with understanding the foundational principles of this dietary approach. Start by acquainting yourself with the types of fruits allowed within the fruitarian diet—ranging from sweet fruits like apples, bananas, and berries to non-sweet varieties like tomatoes, cucumbers, and avocados.

Embrace the idea of consuming fruits that can be harvested without harming the plant itself, aligning with the ethos of minimal plant harm.

Begin your fruitarian journey by gradually incorporating more fruits into your daily meals. Experiment with diverse fruits to experience a wide spectrum of flavors, textures, and nutrients.

Prioritize locally sourced, organic, and seasonal fruits whenever possible, ensuring high-quality produce that contributes to your nutritional intake.

Focus on diversity in fruit consumption to obtain a broad range of essential nutrients. Incorporate a colorful variety of fruits rich in vitamins, minerals, antioxidants, and fiber to support overall health and well-being.

Explore different ways to consume fruits—whether in their raw, whole form, blended into smoothies, or combined in creative fruit-based meals.

Gradual adaptation and mindful observation of your body's response to new fruits are crucial. Listen to your body's signals and note any changes in energy levels, digestion, or overall well-being as you introduce different fruits into your diet. This approach allows for a gradual adjustment period, aiding in your body's adaptation to the fruitarian eating style.

Lastly, seek guidance from healthcare professionals or registered dietitians to ensure you're meeting your nutritional needs while embracing a fruit-centric diet.

Consulting with experts can offer personalized advice, supplementation recommendations, and assistance in crafting a balanced meal plan tailored to your individual requirements.

By gradually incorporating diverse, high-quality fruits into your meals and being attentive to your body's responses, you can embark on a journey toward embracing the principles of fruitarian eating while prioritizing nutritional adequacy and well-being.

The Basics of Fruitarianism

Fruitarianism outlines a dietary philosophy centered on consuming fruits that can be harvested without harming the plant itself.

Understanding the types of fruits allowed within this dietary approach and other permissible foods is fundamental to embracing the fruitarian lifestyle.

Sweet Fruits:

Sweet fruits form a significant portion of the fruitarian diet.

These include a wide array of fruits known for their sweetness and palatability, such as:

- **Apples:** Offering a variety of flavors and textures, apples are a versatile addition to a fruitarian diet.

- **Bananas:** Known for their convenience and energy-boosting properties, bananas are a staple among fruitarians.

- **Berries:** Including strawberries, blueberries, raspberries, and blackberries, these nutrient-packed fruits offer antioxidants and vibrant flavors.

- **Citrus Fruits:** Oranges, lemons, limes, and grapefruits provide vitamin C and a tangy zest to the diet.

Non-Sweet Fruits:

In addition to sweet fruits, fruitarianism encompasses non-sweet fruits, which might not possess the same sugar content but are permissible within this dietary approach:

- **Tomatoes:** Classified as a fruit due to their seed-bearing structure, tomatoes offer versatility in culinary creations.

- **Cucumbers:** Often considered a vegetable but botanically a fruit, cucumbers are hydrating and add freshness to meals.

- **Avocados:** Rich in healthy fats, vitamins, and minerals, avocados are prized for their nutritional density.

- **Bell Peppers:** Available in various colors, bell peppers offer vitamin C and crunch to fruitarian dishes.

Nuts and Seeds:

While the focus of a fruitarian diet is on fruits, nuts and seeds are often included in moderation due to their nutritional content:

- **Almonds:** Providing protein, healthy fats, and essential nutrients, almonds are a favored nut among fruitarians.

- **Sunflower Seeds:** Offering a source of protein, vitamins, and minerals, sunflower seeds are commonly included.

- **Pumpkin Seeds:** Rich in zinc and magnesium, pumpkin seeds add texture and nutritional value to meals.

Other Permissible Foods:

Occasionally, some fruitarians might incorporate certain plant-based foods that align with the principle of minimal harm to plants, such as select leafy greens, herbs, and minimal quantities of specific vegetables that can be harvested without damaging the plant.

Understanding and embracing the range of permissible fruits, nuts, seeds, and occasional plant-based foods allows individuals to craft a diverse and nutritious diet within the parameters of fruitarianism while aiming to minimize harm to plants.

Choosing High-Quality Fruits

Selecting high-quality fruits is integral to deriving optimal nutrition and flavor in a fruitarian diet. Consider these tips when choosing ripe, fresh, and seasonal fruits:

1. Appearance:

- **Color and Texture:** Look for fruits with vibrant, natural colors and smooth, unblemished skins. Avoid fruits with bruises, cuts, or discoloration.

- **Firmness:** Depending on the fruit type, seek firmness without being too hard or overly soft. Some fruits like apples and oranges should feel heavy for their size.

2. Smell:

- **Fragrance:** A pleasant, sweet aroma often indicates ripeness. Fruits like melons and berries should emit a characteristic fruity scent.

3. Sound:

- **Tapping or Thumping:** Certain fruits, such as watermelons, can produce a hollow sound when tapped or thumped, indicating ripeness.

4. Seasonality:

- **Know Seasonal Varieties:** Opt for fruits that are in season. Seasonal fruits are often fresher, more flavorful, and have higher nutritional value.

- **Local Produce:** Consider purchasing fruits from local farmers' markets or grocers for fresher, seasonal options.

5. Touch:

- **Sensitivity to Touch:** For delicate fruits like peaches or avocados, gentle pressure near the stem or bottom can indicate ripeness. They should yield slightly to gentle pressure without being too soft.

6. Ripening Stages:

- **Ready-to-Eat vs. Ripening at Home:** Determine whether the fruit needs time to ripen at home or if it's ready for immediate consumption. Some fruits, like bananas or avocados, continue to ripen after purchase.

7. Storage and Handling:

- **Proper Storage:** Store fruits properly to maintain freshness. Some fruits require refrigeration, while others are best stored at room temperature.

- **Handling Carefully:** Handle fruits gently to prevent bruising or damage, maintaining their quality.

8. Variety and Experimentation:

- **Explore New Varieties:** Experiment with different varieties of fruits to diversify flavors and nutrient intake.

- **Local and Organic Options:** Consider organic or pesticide-free options, especially for fruits with edible skins.

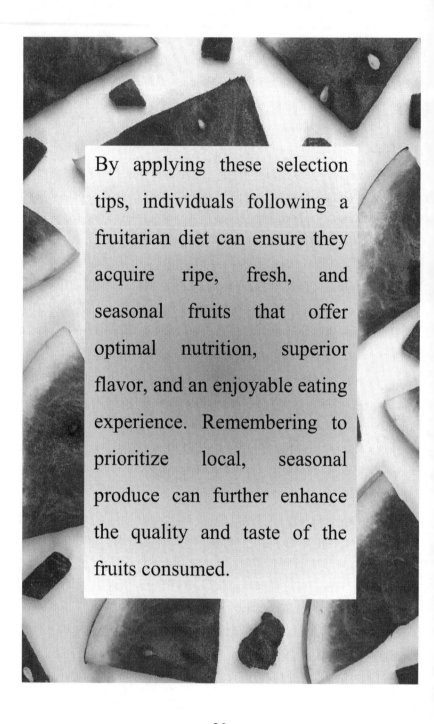

By applying these selection tips, individuals following a fruitarian diet can ensure they acquire ripe, fresh, and seasonal fruits that offer optimal nutrition, superior flavor, and an enjoyable eating experience. Remembering to prioritize local, seasonal produce can further enhance the quality and taste of the fruits consumed.

Preparing Fruitarian Meals

Preparing meals as a fruitarian involves creativity and a focus on utilizing a variety of fruits, nuts, seeds, and occasional permissible plant-based foods.

Here's a guide on preparing fruitarian meals:

1. Fruit-Based Breakfasts:

- **Smoothie Bowls:** Blend different fruits like bananas, berries, and mangoes as a base, top with nuts, seeds, and additional fruits for a colorful and nutrient-packed breakfast.

- **Fruit Salads:** Combine a variety of fruits like melons, citrus, and kiwi for a refreshing morning salad. Add nuts or seeds for texture and additional nutrients.

2. Lunch and Dinner Creations:

- **Raw Veggie Noodles:** Spiralize zucchini or cucumber into "noodles," top with fresh tomato-based or avocado-based sauces, and add herbs or nuts for flavor.

- Raw Wraps: Use large lettuce leaves or collard greens as wraps, fill with sliced fruits, avocado, nuts, and seeds for a crunchy and satisfying meal.

3. Snacks and Treats:

- Fruit Snacks: Keep bite-sized portions of fruits like apples, grapes, or berries for quick and easy snacking throughout the day.

- Dessert Options: Create simple fruit-based desserts like frozen banana "ice cream," fruit sorbets, or fruit salads drizzled with honey or nut butter.

4. Beverages and Drinks:

- Smoothies and Juices: Experiment with various fruit combinations for nutritious and refreshing beverages. Add seeds or nuts for added nutrition.

- Fruit Infusions: Infuse water with sliced fruits like citrus or berries for a flavorful, hydrating drink.

5. Experimentation and Variety:

- Explore Recipes: Look for fruit-based recipes online or in fruitarian cookbooks to diversify meal options and discover new combinations.

- **Creative Combinations:** Mix and match different fruits, nuts, and seeds to create unique and satisfying meals that cater to individual taste preferences.

6. Meal Planning and Prepping:

- **Plan Ahead:** Prepare fruits in advance by washing, cutting, and storing them to have readily available ingredients for quick meals.

- **Balance and Nutrient Consideration:** Ensure meals offer a variety of fruits and incorporate nuts or seeds to balance nutritional needs.

Fruitarian meal preparation involves experimenting with various fruit combinations, incorporating nuts, seeds, and occasionally permissible plant-based foods. Embrace creativity in meal planning to ensure a diverse, nutrient-rich, and satisfying fruitarian diet.

FRUITARIANS ARE HEALTHY PEOPLE BECAUSE FRUITS HELP REDUCE THE PACE OF AGING, DETOXIFY AND CLEANSE, BOOST IMMUNE AND BALANCE HORMONE.

CHAPTER 3

Nutritious Fruitarian Breakfast Recipes

1. Tropical Smoothie Bowl

Nutritional Information (per serving):

- Calories: 320 kcal

- Carbohydrates: 80g

- Fiber: 10g

- Protein: 4g

Prep Time: 10 minutes

Ingredients:

- 1 frozen banana

- 1 cup frozen mango chunks

- ½ cup pineapple chunks

- ½ cup coconut water or almond milk

- Toppings: Sliced kiwi, shredded coconut, chia seeds

Method:

1. Blend frozen banana, mango, pineapple, and coconut water (or almond milk) until smooth.

2. Pour into a bowl and top with sliced kiwi, shredded coconut, and chia seeds.

2. Berry Fruit Salad

Nutritional Information (per serving):

- Calories: 120 kcal

- Carbohydrates: 30g

- Fiber: 12g

- Protein: 3g

Prep Time: 10 minutes

Ingredients:

- 1 cup strawberries (sliced)

- 1 cup blueberries

- 1 cup raspberries

- 1 tablespoon fresh mint leaves (chopped)

- 1 tablespoon lemon juice

Method:

1. Combine all the berries in a bowl.

2. Add chopped mint leaves and lemon juice, toss gently to combine.

3. Banana-Oat Pancakes

Nutritional Information (per serving):

- Calories: 240 kcal

- Carbohydrates: 50g

- Fiber: 6g

- Protein: 6g

Prep Time: 15 minutes

Ingredients:

- 2 ripe bananas (mashed)

- 1 cup rolled oats

- 1 teaspoon baking powder

- ½ teaspoon cinnamon

- Coconut oil (for cooking)

Method:

1. Mash bananas in a bowl, add oats, baking powder, and cinnamon. Mix well.

2. Heat coconut oil in a pan, spoon pancake batter onto the pan, cook until golden brown on both sides.

4. Apple-Cinnamon Breakfast Quinoa

Nutritional Information (per serving):

- Calories: 280 kcal

- Carbohydrates: 60g

- Fiber: 8g

- Protein: 6g

Prep Time: 20 minutes (if quinoa is pre-cooked)

Ingredients:

- 1 cup cooked quinoa

- 1 apple (diced)

- 1 tablespoon maple syrup

- ½ teaspoon cinnamon

- Almond slices (for garnish)

Method:

1. In a bowl, mix cooked quinoa, diced apple, maple syrup, and cinnamon.

2. Serve in a bowl, garnish with almond slices.

5. Citrusy Chia Seed Pudding

Nutritional Information (per serving):

- Calories: 180 kcal

- Carbohydrates: 30g

- Fiber: 12g

- Protein: 4g

Prep Time: 10 minutes (+ chilling time)

Ingredients:

- ¼ cup chia seeds

- 1 cup orange juice

- ½ teaspoon vanilla extract

- Sliced oranges for garnish

Method:

1. Mix chia seeds, orange juice, and vanilla extract in a bowl. Let it sit for 15-20 minutes or overnight until it thickens.

2. Serve in a bowl or jar, garnish with sliced oranges.

Absolutely, here are five more nutritious fruitarian breakfast recipes:

6. Avocado-Berry Breakfast Bowl

Nutritional Information (per serving):

- Calories: 320 kcal

- Carbohydrates: 28g

- Fiber: 15g

- Protein: 7g

Prep Time: 10 minutes

Ingredients:

- 1 ripe avocado

- 1 cup mixed berries (such as strawberries, blueberries, and raspberries)

- 2 tablespoons hemp seeds

- 1 tablespoon honey or agave syrup

Method:

1. Mash the avocado in a bowl.

2. Top with mixed berries, hemp seeds, and drizzle honey or agave syrup.

7. Pineapple-Coconut Chia Pudding

Nutritional Information (per serving):

- Calories: 280 kcal

- Carbohydrates: 30g

- Fiber: 18g

- Protein: 6g

Prep Time: 15 minutes (+ chilling time)

Ingredients:

- ½ cup chia seeds

- 2 cups coconut milk

- 1 cup diced pineapple

- 2 tablespoons shredded coconut

Method:

1. Mix chia seeds and coconut milk, let it sit for 10 minutes, stirring occasionally.

2. Layer chia pudding with diced pineapple in serving glasses, top with shredded coconut.

8. Mango-Almond Butter Toast

Nutritional   Information (per serving):

- Calories: 320 kcal

- Carbohydrates: 45g

- Fiber: 8g

- Protein: 9g

Prep Time: 10 minutes

Ingredients:

- 2 slices of whole-grain bread

- 2 tablespoons almond butter

- 1 ripe mango (sliced)

Method:

1. Toast the bread slices.

2. Spread almond butter on the toast and top with slices of ripe mango.

9. Kiwi-Melon Breakfast Skewers

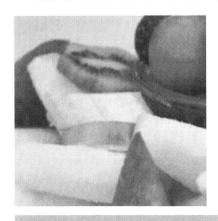

Nutritional Information (per serving):

- Calories: 110 kcal

- Carbohydrates: 28g

- Fiber: 5g

- Protein: 2g

Prep Time: 10 minutes

Ingredients:

- 2 kiwis (peeled and sliced)

- 1 cup cubed watermelon

- 1 cup cubed honeydew melon

- Wooden skewers

Method:

1. Thread kiwi, watermelon, and honeydew melon alternately onto skewers.

2. Serve immediately or refrigerate for a refreshing breakfast option.

10. Berry-Seed Parfait

Nutritional Information (per serving):

- Calories: 180 kcal

- Carbohydrates: 25g

- Fiber: 8g

- Protein: 6g

Prep Time: 15 minutes

Ingredients:

- 1 cup mixed berries (strawberries, blueberries, raspberries)

- 1 cup dairy-free yogurt

- 2 tablespoons mixed seeds (such as chia, flax, sunflower)

Method:

1. Layer berries and yogurt in a glass or bowl.

2. Top with mixed seeds for added crunch and nutritional value.

11. Baked Yogurt With Honey Cinnamon Grilled Fruits

The recipe is very simple and requires just a few simple ingredients. You can use any topping you like from simple fruit compote to grilled fruits or you can serve it as it is.

Prep Time: 30 minutes

Ingredients:

1 cup Curd (Dahi / Yogurt)

1 cup Fresh cream

1 cup Condensed Milk

3/4 teaspoon Vanilla Extract

For the topping:

1 cup Pineapple , sliced

1 Pears, sliced

2 Peaches, sliced

2 Plum, sliced

4 Strawberries, sliced

1 Mango (Ripe), sliced

1 tablespoon Butter (Salted)

1/2 teaspoon Cinnamon Powder (Dalchini)

Methods:

First pre-heat the oven to 160 degree Celsius

Add the yogurt to a mixing bowl and whisk.

Add the cream, condensed milk and vanilla extract if using. Whisk till everything blends well.

Pour the mixture into 5-6 ramekins.

Make a water bath by pouring water in a baking tray till it is half filled.

Place the ramekins in the water bath and bake for about 18-20 minutes or till the mixture is just set.

Cool and refrigerate for a couple of hours.

To make the topping, heat and brush a grill pan with the butter.

Place the fruit slices on the pan and grill for 1-2 minutes, till you see grill marks on the slice. This time may change depending on the fruit used.

Whisk the honey and cinnamon in a small bowl.Brush it on the fruit slices.Take the fruits slices off the heat.

Cool completely and place them on top of the cold baked yogurt and serve.

12. Thai Grilled Pineapple

Very ideal dessert for parties and potlucks as it does not involve much cooking time and can be served at room temperature. It also does not need any region specific ingredients except for the palm sugar which can be replaced with normal sugar.

Prep Time: 20 minutes

Ingredients:

1 Pineapple, sliced to inch thick (about 6 slices)

1 tablespoon Fresh coconut, grated

3 tablespoon Butter (Salted)

3 tablespoon Lemon juice

1-1/2 teaspoon Palm sugar

6 teaspoon Hung Curd (Greek Yogurt)

Methods:

Toast the coconut in a Shallow-fry pan until it lightly browns and aromatic. Set aside in a bowl.

Heat butter in the same pan and let it melt completely.

Place the pineapple slices in the melted butter, sprinkle palm sugar and lemon juice on it. You can omit sugar if the pineapple slices are sweet enough for you. Flip them immediately once so that the palm sugar and lemon juice gets evenly coated on both the sides.

Cook the pineapple, stirring and flipping at regular intervals until the palm sugar is dissolved.

Once the palm sugar is dissolved, keep it for about 3 minutes on each side (low medium flame) so that the pineapple is fried nicely.

Place 2 pineapples in each bowl and add a dollop of fresh and creamy yogurt.

Sprinkle with fried coconut and serve.

13. Fruit Sandwich

Perfect to serve as an after school snack to your kids. You can also serve it as an evening snack with a cup of coffee.

Prep Time: 15 minutes

Ingredients:

3 Whole Wheat Brown Bread

2 Ripe Bananas, peeled and sliced

2 Pineapple, sliced thin

1 Apple, or chickoo, sliced

2 tablespoon Jam, Mixed fruit

Methods:

To prepare Fruit Sandwich Recipe, get all the ingredients handy. Apply jam to one side of 2 bread slices.

To assemble the sandwich, take one bread with jam applied and over it place the fruit slices of pineapple, bananas, chickoo or apple in any order. Arrange the fruits slices completely on the bread.

Place another bread slice. The jam side should be facing on the top.

Arrange the sliced fruits again and close the sandwich with a slice to which no jam has been applied.

Grill this fruit sandwich on a Grill sandwich toaster till the topmost slice of bread turns brownish. If you don't like to grill, simply have the sandwich as it is.

To serve, cut the sandwich into 2 triangles and serve.

14. Sweet Mixed Fruits and Granola

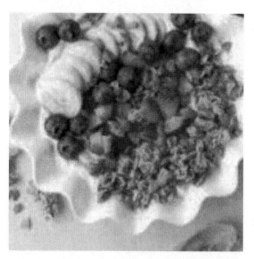

A variation of sweet burritos that are perfect for the morning rush. To make this more healthy add nuts of your choice.

Prep Time: 15 minutes

Ingredients:

2 Whole Wheat Flour Tortilla

1/4 cup Strawberries , thinly sliced

1/4 cup Ripe Bananas , thinly sliced

1/4 cup Peaches , thinly sliced

1/4 cup Fresh raspberries , roughly chopped

1 teaspoon Honey

1/3 cup Granola , or mixed nuts

4 tablespoon Britannia Cream Cheese , softened

Methods:

In a small bowl add all the fruits and stir in the honey, make sure fruits are coated well.

Warm up the Tortillas on a skillet and place it on a serving platter.

Spread the cream cheese on the tortillas leaving an inch from the border.

Arrange the prepared fruit mix one half down the center of each tortilla, sprinkle the granola.

Fold the sides of each tortilla and roll to make a wrap (should look like burrito).

15. Easy Creamy Fruit Trifle Recipe

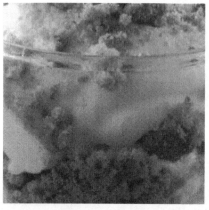 The creamy fruit pudding can be had at any time of the day, in the evenings or even as a post-lunch dessert, and the taste can be varied depending on the kind of fruits that go into the drink.

Prep Time: 20 minutes

Ingredients:

200 grams Hung Curd (Greek Yogurt)

100 ml Fresh cream , chilled

3 tablespoons Sugar , powdered

1 Strawberry Compote , recipe

5 to 6 Marie Biscuit , crumbled, (I used oats biscuits)

Methods:

First whisk the cream and sugar until thick with soft peaks. Using an electric whisk, helps quicken the process.

Gradually add in the greek yogurt and whisk until just combined. Keep this aside.

Make sure you have the strawberry compote ready; you can also substitute this trifle with fresh fruits like kiwi, mangoes and strawberries.

We will now serve them in individual glasses; add a few spoons of oat crumble to the bottom of the glass; next alternatively add in the whipped yogurt and the fruits. Finally top it with the oat crumble

Refrigerate the Creamy Fruit Trifle for 4 to 5 hours before you are ready to serve.

16. Detox Blueberry Salad

This recipe, helps you lose weight, increase your energy, and the most importantly, reset your frame of mind, end craving and flush out the toxins in your system, so it is easier to eat healthy and live better.

Prep Time: 20 minutes

Methods:

Prepare the dressing for the salad. Place all ingredients mentioned under 'For dressing' in a big bowl and mix everything well.

Put all the ingredients in a mixer and pulse them to obtain a smooth paste.

The next step is to make the salad. Place all the vegetables in a large bowl and toss them to combine.

Pour the dressing over the salad and mix to combine. Garnish it with toasted almonds and flax seeds.

Serve Detox Blueberry Salad on its own for a healthy and light dinner.

17. Fruit Kesari

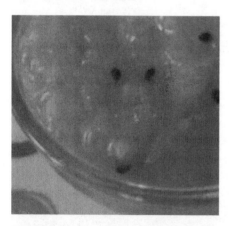

Fruit Kesari Recipe is a delicious semolina Pudding made with Dragon fruit. The dragon fruit cooked in ghee along with roasted millets, sugar, cardamom ,garnished with cashew nuts and finally flavored with rose water brings out great taste and flavor to the kesari.

Prep Time: 15 minutes

Ingredients:

1/2 cup Pink Flesh Dragon Fruit/Pitaya , pulp

1/3 cup Foxtail Millet

1/4 cup Brown Sugar (Demerara Sugar)

1 tablespoon Rose water

1/4 cup Ghee

1 teaspoon Cardamom Powder (Elaichi)

1/4 cup Cashew nuts , broken

Methods:

Cut the dragon fruit into half. We actually need less than 1/2 for a 1/2 cup pulp.

Scoop it out and chop them into big chunks.

Grind the dragon fruit without adding any water.

You will see the seeds still visible, it is just fine as we need that nutty flavor in the final dish.

There should not be any chunks of dragonfruit left out.

Take a non-stick pan and dry roast the mixed millets until a nice aroma comes.

Allow it to cool.

Add them in the mixer and blending it into coarse powder consistency.

It need to reach the sooji rava consistency (almost)

Take the non-stick pan and in medium flame gas, add 1/2 tablespoon ghee and roast the cashew nuts.

Once roasted, take the cashew nuts and keep it separately.

In the same pan, add dragon fruit pulp first and then water and let it boil.

Once it boils, reduce the gas to low flame and add the millets and keep stirring the kesari continuously without forming lumps.

Once the dragon fruit kesari becomes thick and the millets are cooked add cardamon powder, sugar and give it a mix.

At this stage you might see some water coming but it is still fine the dragon fruit kesari will get thicker.

Once the sugar is mixed and melted add cashew nuts and remaining ghee.

Finally add the rosewater and give the kesari mix and turn off the heat.

18. Oats Yogurt Parfait with Fruits

The word "parfait" is a French word meaning 'frozen dessert'. Parfait has become one of the most popular breakfast or dessert option which is made with yogurt.

Prep Time: 20 minutes

Ingredients:

3 tablespoons Hung Curd (Greek Yogurt)

1-1/2 tablespoons Instant Oats (Oatmeal) , Instant

1/2 teaspoon Vanilla Extract

1/2 tablespoon Honey , adjustable

1/4 cup Water

1-1/2 tablespoon Wheat Flakes (Cereal)

Fresh fruits, of preference, chopped (I have used grapes & strawberries)

Methods:

Add oats and water in a pan and boil until cooked.

Add vanilla essence and honey, stir once and allow it to cool.

Place the cooked oats in a tall glass, add yogurt.

Top it up with wheat flakes which will give it the Oats Yogurt Parfait with Fruits a crunchy taste.

Add a few cut fruits.

Repeat the layering till you fill the glass 3/4 th. Top the parfait with more fruits.

Serve this Oats Yogurt Parfait with Fruits recipe immediately to enjoy the crunchy goodness of wheat flakes, the sweet cooked oats and fruits.

Serve Oats Yogurt Parfait with Fruits Recipe with a hot cup of Masala Chai for breakfast.

19. Savory Melon Salad with Ginger & Mint

Made from seasonal fruits likes watermelon and muskmelon and combined with a tangy ginger dressing makes this salad refreshing and delicious.

Prep Time: 25 minutes

Ingredients:

1/2 Watermelon, cut into cubes

1/2 Musk Melon, cut into cubes

2 Cucumbers, peeled and diced

Mint Leaves (Pudina), a small bunch

Ingredients for the dressing:

2 teaspoon Extra Virgin Olive Oil

Lemon juice, from 2 lemons

2 teaspoon Honey

1 inch Ginger , grated

1 Tabasco Original - Hot Sauce, drizzle over as per preference

Salt, as per taste

Methods:

First cube or ball the melons to bite size pieces.

Add the cut melons into a large salad mixing bowl.

Our next step is to combine all the ingredients for the dressing. Add the dressing ingredients into a small bowl and using a fork whisk all the ingredients together until well combined.

You can prepare the dressing ahead of time and store it in a small jar in the refrigerator and use as desired.

Once the salad dressing is ready, pour it over the cut melons and give the salad a good stir. Stir in the chopped mint leaves and feta cheese.

Serve savory melon salad along with grilled sub sandwich with paneer & roasted vegetables for a light summer lunch.

20. Spiced Coconut Oatmeal with Assorted Fruits

This is a simple homemade breakfast recipe made with healthy ingredients. Sometimes when we are in a hurry to go out or if we are looking for some quick and healthy breakfast to grab, this recipe will surely help you out to keep you fit and energetic.

Prep Time: 25 minutes

Ingredients:

1/2 cup Instant Oats (Oatmeal)

1 cup Lukewarm Water

1/4 cup Coconut milk

2 teaspoons Honey

1/4 teaspoon Cinnamon Powder (Dalchini)

1/8 teaspoon Dry ginger powder

2 Ripe Bananas, sliced

3 Dates, sliced

2 tablespoon Anardana Powder (Pomegranate Seed Powder)

2 tablespoons Walnuts

Salt, a pinch

Methods:

Start by boiling the oats with water, pinch of salt and spice powders in a saucepan till it thickens and gets cooked. This will take about 10- 12 minutes.

Take it out from heat and transfer it into a serving bowl.

Add coconut milk , top it up with fruits, and drizzle some honey and give it a stir.

Serve spiced coconut oatmeal with assorted fruits topped with some more fruits during a quick morning breakfast along with cantaloupe (Melon) Juice.

CONCLUSION

In drawing the final curtain on the Fruitarian Diet Cookbook, it encapsulates more than just a compilation of recipes; it's a journey towards optimal health and culinary exploration.

This comprehensive collection has unlocked the vast potential of fruits in crafting delectable dinners, showcasing a myriad of inventive, nutritious, and enticing dishes. From zesty fruit salads to innovative fruit-based stews and sushi rolls, each recipe embarks on a flavorful adventure that celebrates the natural sweetness and vitality of fruits. This cookbook embodies more than just meals; it symbolizes a lifestyle that embraces the bountiful offerings of nature. By choosing the Fruitarian Diet, individuals embark on a path abundant in health, vitality, and satisfaction. It's an exploration into a world of flavors, colors, and textures that celebrate the wholesome goodness of fruits. Beyond its culinary aspects, this cookbook encourages a profound appreciation for nature's gifts, promoting mindfulness and a more conscious approach to eating. It's a testament to the fact that healthful living can be both delicious and rewarding. The Fruitarian Diet Cookbook serves as an invaluable guide, providing the tools and inspiration for individuals to infuse their dinners with vibrant, nutrient-rich fruit-based creations, transforming mealtimes into delightful, healthful experiences.

If You desire optimal health, slower aging, and disease prevention, consider embracing a balanced lifestyle. Healthy eating, regular exercise, and adequate rest contribute significantly to overall well-being. Making conscious choices in nutrition, engaging in physical activities you enjoy, and prioritizing sufficient sleep are key components. Small, consistent changes pave the way for a healthier, more vibrant life.

Printed in Great Britain
by Amazon